Lock Pick

Complete Beginners & Intermediates

Complete Visual Guide to Lock Picking for Beginners and Intermediates For 2020 and Beyond

Introduction

Let's visualize something together:

It's been a long day at work, and you've just arrived home late at night, tired and ready for a good night's sleep. You start digging into your pockets, looking for your keys. Suddenly, you realize you've lost your keys.

Trying to trace your steps leads to a dead-end, breaking into your home is not an ideal solution, and it's too late to find a locksmith. The only viable option you have left is to seek refuge at a friend's place for the night and wait to call a locksmith to pick the lock the next day.

If you have experienced such a situation, you know how exasperating it can be. If you'd like to avoid such situations in the future, you need to learn how to pick a lock, an endeavor that, as you shall soon learn from this guide, is as easy as it looks in the movies.

This guide will teach you:

✓ The benefits of learning how to pick locks,

✓ The basics of lock picking, including the various parts of a lock, types of locks, the tools used in lock picking, and tons more,

✓ Various DIY lock picking approaches you can use to pick different types of locks,

And so much more.

Let's start with looking at why you should learn how to pick locks:

Table of Content

Chapter 1: The Advantages of Learning How to Pick Locks

A common misbelief is the only reason why anyone would want to learn how to pick locks is to break into other people's homes. That's not the case.

There're a couple of positive reasons why you should learn how to pick a lock. Here are some of the most prominent ones:

#: *To know how secure you are from intruders*

Usually, you use locks to keep your loved ones and possessions safe.

After picking locks around your house, you will realize that all they do is create a fake perception of safety and security. Most locks only make you feel safe without offering any actual protection. If a motivated intruder wanted to gain access to your house, the locks you use are unlikely to keep out such an intruder.

Knowing how secure or insecure your locks are will help you go the extra mile to keep your house safe by adding an extra layer of security.

#: *You acquire a handy skill*

As stated earlier, getting locked out of your car or house can be quite frustrating. Learning how to pick a lock will help you save a lot of money that you would have otherwise used to hire a locksmith. Should a friend or family member lose his or her keys, you can also help out.

Lock picking is a handy skill that can even help you save someone's life. Picture this:

A friend or family member calls you with a call for help. Getting to the person's house, you find the door locked. You peep through a window or keyhole and see the person lying on the ground, struggling to breathe.

At this point, calling 911 is not the quickest option; you need to give the person first aid before the ambulance gets there. First, however, you need to gain access to the premise as quickly as possible. Picking the lock can come in handy at such a point. Sure, there are other options such as kicking down the door or breaking a window, but picking the lock takes a few seconds, is safer, and does not leave a lot of damage that will probably take monetary resources to solve.

#: It's fun and cool

Picking a lock certainly has a cool factor. Imagine how mind-blown your friends will be when you pick their locks and help them open their doors. The idea that you can get into any door without a key will make you feel as powerful as a master spy!

You can also use this skill as a hobby. Additionally, if you become very good at it, you can join contests and events to test your lock-picking skills against other people —if you win, you may even earn a few bucks while at it.

Although these are the most prominent benefits of learning how to pick locks, they're not the only ones. Others include:

✓ You can get out of hairy situations,

✓ It'll help you become more focused because picking a lock takes focus,

✓ Lock picking is also a marketable skill.

Now that you know the benefits of lock picking, let's talk about locks and how they work:

Chapter 2:   Lock Picking 101, An Introduction

Learning to pick a lock is not rocket science; any determined person can learn how to do it with ease because lock picking is simple:

In simple terms, lock picking is a way to open locks without using the original key or destroying the lock.

There are various ways to do so, but most revolve around mimicking the way a key works, which means to master the craft, the first thing you need to learn is how locks work:

How a Key Works

To pick a lock by mimicking the key, you need to understand how a lock and key work so that you can understand the mechanisms behind it.

Today, we have many types of locks. Most of them look different in terms of appearance and place of application. However, one kind of lock beats them all: the *pin tumbler lock*. This type of lock dates back to early Egypt, making it over 6,000 years old.

Over 90% of the locks in the world use the pin tumbler mechanism, making learning how to pick this kind of lock your first stop. Additionally, once you learn how to pick a pin tumbler lock, you can apply the skill in one form or the other on other lock types.

Parts Of The Pin Tumbler Lock

The pin tumbler lock mechanism has six main manipulatable parts:

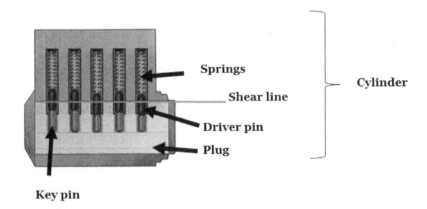

1: The cylinder

Also called the body of the lock, the housing, or the shell, the cylinder is simply a container that houses the functional components of the lock. This part typically slides into the padlock or door and also creates the upper section of the shear line.

2: The plug

This part is a cylinder where you insert the key; it rotates freely inside the main cylinder when you insert the correct key. The plug creates the lower part of the shear line. On the other side of the keyhole, it holds a tailpiece or cam that retracts, which, when rotated, opens the lock.

3: The shear line

Simply put, the Shear line is the physical gap between the plug and the housing. It is a vital lock picking part since it is a conceptual line that allows the plug to rotate.

With the line obstructed, the housing and plug lock into each other, thereby barring the plug from turning. The plug can only rotate freely when the sheer line is free from obstructions.

4: Springs

The springs have two functions inside a lock. First, they are responsible for pushing down the pins into the plug. Their second function is to push the key pins against a key so that they can read the notches. Without springs, the pins can remain stuck at any point in the pin chamber, thereby rendering the lock useless.

5: *Driver pins*

These are the upper set of pins in a lock; they're responsible for keeping a lock in the lock position. They work by obstructing the sheer line, hence hindering rotation of the plug. Driver pins are usually of the same size as opposed to key pins.

6: *Key pins*

Key pins are the lower set of pins; they are responsible for reading the notches on a key by using pins of different length and cutting patterns on a key that match the lengths of the key pins. That explains why a key has low spots and high spots.

When you insert a key into the plug, each key pin moves upward flush with the lock's Shear line, hence clearing the sheer line of any obstruction. The driver pins, on the other hand, become forced out of the plug and stay flush with the shear line, which allows you to rotate the key and disengage the lock.

These are the most critical parts of a lock. If you master them, you will be well on your way to being a master lock picker.

The next part of your learning journey is to understand the various types of locks:

Chapter 3: Types Of Locks

The first step to getting good at picking locks is to understand the types of locks and the common factor that binds them all.

While there're many types of locks, the main ones fall into six categories:

✓ Mortise locks,

✓ Cam locks,

✓ Padlocks,

✓ Knobs,

✓ Electronic locks,

✓ Deadbolts, and

1: Knob locks

These are the most common types of locks used for doors, particularly room entrance doors. These locks are not ideal for external doors since they offer low security.

Their lock mechanisms are in the knob instead of the door, which means an intruder can use simple tools such as a wrench or hammer to knock the knob off and pliers to rotate the locking mechanism. These types of locks are also easy to pick.

2: Cam locks

These locks are common on furniture, lockboxes, filing cabinets, and other low-security storage. Cam locks use a small metallic tailpiece referred to as a cam, the piece that a key rotates to either lock or unlock the lock.

Cam locks mostly use the tubular locking mechanism or the pin tumbler mechanism, which are both very simple to pick.

3: Deadbolt lock

These locks are the ones often used on external doors to residential homes. Their most common pairing is a knob lock for an added layer of security. They use a rotating cylinder that drives a bolt into the frame of a door. You have to rotate the cylinder once more to retract the bolt.

Although these locks are highly resilient to shimming and brute force attacks, they are easy to pick because they use the pin tumbler locking mechanism.

Deadbolt locks come in two variations:

✓ Single cylinder

✓ Double cylinder.

You can only open Single cylinder variations with a key from one side, mostly the exterior side of the door, with the other side operated using a knob. Double cylinder deadbolt locks are operatable with a key from both sides.

4: Padlocks

Padlocks are usually portable and never permanently attached to anything. They use a shackle to secure items. There are two types of padlocks:

✓ Combination padlocks, and,

✓ Keyed

These two types of padlocks have three main components:

✓ The locking mechanism,

✓ The shackle, and

✓ The body

As the name suggests, keyed padlocks use a key to lock or unlock. Keyed padlocks can either be non-key-retaining or key retaining.

For key retaining padlocks, you cannot remove the key when you have the padlock unlocked. For non-key-retaining models, you can remove the key when the lock is open.

Keyed padlocks can be re-keyable, meaning you can replace the cylinder of the padlock with another one, thus using a new key.

Combination padlocks, on the other hand, use a series of numbers that open a lock when you enter the "pin" correctly.

Padlocks are easy to compromise because you can brute force them —perhaps by using a drill, hammers, and bolt cutters. They are also very susceptible to shimming and lock picking. Although they seem "more secure," Combination locks are anything but because you can use combination cracking to pick them.

5: Mortise locks

Mortise locks are strong locks often used on external doors. They are available in both heavy and light duty.

Heavy-duty models are ideal for commercial applications because they can withstand frequent usage without breaking down. This kind of lock requires cutting a pocket into the edge of the door.

It may have a couple of components, including the escutcheons, trims, lock body, and levers. It also comes with a mortise cylinder threaded into the body of the mortise lock. The mortise cylinder has a small groove on its edge, fastened with two screw sets responsible for holding it firmly in place.

6: Electronic locks

Electronic locks use a different concept altogether. Since most of them do not require a physical metallic key, they are more secure against lock picking.

Instead of using a key, some use passwords or passphrases, plastic cards that look like credit cards, biometric scanners, iris scanners, and in some cases, disposable security tokens to add that extra layer of security.

Electronic locks come in different shapes, sizes, and mechanisms, thus making them harder to exploit.

Having covered the various types of locks available, we can discuss the tools you need to pick locks:

Chapter 4: Lock Picking Tools

With so many gizmos and lock picks out there, choosing your first set can become a real challenge. That doesn't have to be the case. The truth is that you do not need all the tools you can get your hands on to get started in lock picking.

Despite owning an extensive collection of lock picking tools, even pro-lock pickers use a handful of tools. Some of them even prefer using simple tools fashioned out of household items such as bobby pins.

Getting lock picking tools is ideal, yes, but not necessary. You can get by well without them. That mentioned, here are the most basic tools you may need:

Basic Tools

The most basic lock picking tools are

Hooks

Also called feeler picks, these are pointy and narrow lock picks that work in a very precise and pinpoint manner inside a lock. The preciseness factor makes them a perfect choice for single pin picking in cases where you need to feel the pins inside the lock and manipulate each one on its own.

We have different hook varieties with different styles, shapes, and lengths. However, all of them work with the same goal in mind: to manipulate one pin at a time.

1: Half-diamond picks

This type of lock pick works in the same way as a feeler hook.

2: Half-moon picks

This type of pick works best for locks that use metal wafers in their cylinders instead of pins. The roundedness of the tip allows it to navigate inside the lock without getting trapped in the wafers.

Wafer locks are common on low-level security locks like mailboxes and some vehicle brands. You can also unlock these types of locks using the raking method.

All the tools in this category are available in many other forms. For instance, feelers may have a variation in their curvature. You may also find other kits that include two-sided tools that exhibit characteristics in this category that can you can use to pick locks that have two rows of pins simultaneously.

Rakes

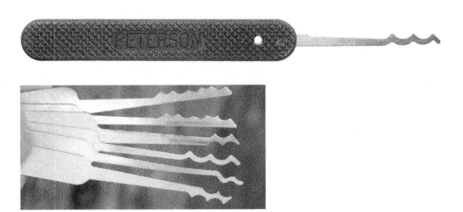

Rakes are usually erratic-looking because they have a lot of bumps and humps that help them maximize the number of pins they can manipulate in the shortest time possible.

The market has a wide variety of rakes —just as is the case for hooks— but each will have a specific success rate on a given lock. However, you should note that you can't use the raking to pick some locks.

We have two major categories of raking tools: snake rakes & city rakes. Snake rakes have a curvy form that resembles a snake, while city rakes have teeth referred to as rakes —they usually resemble a saw.

City rake

Snake rake

Tension wrench

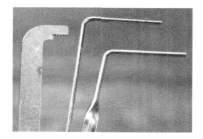

A tension wrench is a critical lock picking tool you should own as a lock picker. Without this basic-looking tool, lock picking is impossible. We use the tool to apply pressure to the lock's plug, hence biding the pins.

There're several designs for tension wrenches, each meant for different keyways and lock sizes. The most basic one is the straight tension wrench, which has an L-shape.

Besides the basic tools you need to start lock picking, you can acquire advanced tools to improve your expertise.

Advanced Lock Picking Tools

Below are some advanced lock picking tools you can use:

Lock picking gun

1: Manual lock pick gun

Also called a snap gun, a lock pick gun is a tool used to force a pin tumbler lock to open rapidly without a key.

Unlike other tools in this list, the lock picking gun is not small or pocket-sized. It's a fairly large tool that you can use to rake a lock without much effort. On a positive note, it is quite fast and will help you gain entry with the least effort.

Here's how it works:

Unlike the traditional way of lock picking, the lock pick gun does not use trial- and error methods; it uses the laws of physics, specifically the transfer of energy.

Firstly, you insert a thin rod made of steel into the lock. When you press the trigger, the rod pushes against all the lock pins quickly. This action allows a momentary freeing of the lock's cylinder, which in turn enables you to turn it. The strong impact generated pushes all the driver pins out of the lock cylinder without actually moving the key pins.

The kinetic energy generated from the gun moves through the key pins to the driver pins, with the springs absorbing it, which, in turn, results in a momentary period when the cylinder becomes unobstructed.

Although a snap gun opens a lock very quickly, the sharp impact it generates is more likely to cause damage to the mechanism of a lock; in worst-case scenarios, it can render the original key unusable.

2: Electric lock pick gun

These types of lock pick guns use either an electromagnet or a motor to oscillate a needle continuously.

You insert the needle into the lock to fit under all the key pins. It then vibrates, aiming to resonate at a frequency that can cause all the driver pins to move above the shear line, hence allowing you to turn the plug.

Customizable pin locks

A customizable pin tumbler lock has removable pins that you can use to create puzzle-type of locks. It allows you to add harder pins as you progress, hence providing you with an ever-more-complex puzzle that you can solve, and at the same time, improve your skills.

Besides this, you can pick up extra locks, maybe from a reclamation dump, as a way to test your skill on as many varieties of locks as possible.

Lock picking practice sets

Different locksmith training kits are available in the market. Some of these kits are ideal for beginners because they are transparent. The transparency allows you to see the pins as they move inside the lock.

The transparent locks usually come with a key that allows you to see how the key interacts with the pins. This way, you will be able to understand how the lock mechanism works and learn quicker.

Try out keys/Auto jigglers

Try out keys are kind of a set of 'master keys' —to put it simply, they are 'skeleton keys' usually fashioned from tampered stainless steel and come in a set of 10 keys.

Jigglers match many of the common lock pinnings that exist. Creators of these keys take advantage of the existence of many average locks. There is, however, more to jiggler keys.

A jiggler key has to allow movement inside the keyway, which is why most of the keys are thinner than ordinary keys. The shape also allows them to fit into various sizes of keyways without becoming too loose or too tight.

They come in different patterns that help trick the lock into thinking that you are using the correct key. Moreover, some designs are unique to car locks, cabinet locks, or even wafer locks.

Many lock pickers have used these types of keys at auto junk yards to start many different car models for years. The repossession and towing industries are also very fond of using these types of keys. They are handy to have in day-to-day situations, especially if you plan to be a pro-lock picker or locksmith.

Now that we have looked at the various types of lock picking tools available for your consideration, you may be wondering, what factors should I keep in mind when purchasing lock picking tools?

Let's discuss that now:

Buying Lock Picking Tools: Factors to Keep In Mind

Lock picking tools are widely available and inexpensive. Compared to DIY tools, the quality of these tools, thanks to the materials used to make them, make them more valuable. When buying your lock pick tools, keep in mind the following three major considerations:

Fineness

We measure the fineness of a lock picking tool based on the height of your pick blade and the thickness of the blade.

The thickness of the steel used should not exceed 0.7 -0.8 mm. A tool that's thicker than this won't fit smaller keyways; it'll also be difficult to handle, and as a result, interpreting the feedback will be more challenging.

You should also avoid extra thin lock picking tools ranging from 0.3mm to 0.4mm since they have the least amount of strength.

When it comes to the height of the blade, it should not exceed 3mm

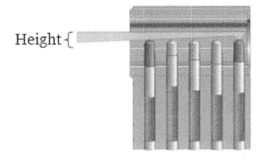

The height of your blade is important because when you insert it into a keyway, it might become difficult to use since, as you try to pick the furthest pin, the blade might contact the other pins behind it.

The strength of the tool

When buying a lock picking tool, it can be quite tricky to assess its strength. If you are not sure how to determine the strength of the tool, go for American or European brands because most of these meet the required standards.

You can also go for other brands, but only if you know the specifics of the steel used during manufacture. Asian brands may be a bit cheaper, but often, they compromise by using substandard materials during the production process.

The tool's ergonomics

Apart from the visual appearance of the tool, the ergonomics of its handle should also be a key consideration because it influences the grip you have on the tool and feedback you receive when picking a lock.

Based on this, avoid handles that have rubber & soft plastic or that are too wide because they tend to suppress feedback, hence making them counterproductive to the lock picking process. Successful lock picking is technique-based, yes, but the feedback you receive from a tool also matters a lot.

The ideal tool to get for good feedback is hard plastic or metal handles that either have or do not have a heat shrink tubing. However, avoid thin bare metal handles, especially if you intend to engage in extended lock picking sessions because it can be painful to hold; such picks also tire your fingers quickly.

A bit about improvised lock picks

Being good at lock picking means you have to learn how to work with whatever tool you have at hand in that moment, which comes handy in situations where you forgot or didn't find it necessary to carry your lock picking set.

Keep in mind that the basic lock picking tools are just small pieces of metal; there's nothing uniquely special to or on them. Therefore, you can create improvised lock picking tools from things such as bobby pins, paper clips, key rings, a hairpin, the underwire from a brassiere, and other small metal objects.

Let's talk about improvised lock picks a bit more deeply:

Chapter 5: DIY Lock Picks

This chapter will teach you how to make a lock pick out of a bobby pin and paper clip. Below are the steps to follow.

How to Make a Lock Pick From A Bobby Pin

Use the following steps to make a lock pick from a bobby pin:

Step 1:

Bobby pins usually have two sides; one of them has wavy curves, while the other side is straight. Both sides have rubber tips at the end. Use your pliers to remove these tips.

Step 2:

Secondly, get rid of the bend on your bobby pin.

Here, your goal is to make the bobby pin as straight as possible. You can use your fingers or your pliers to achieve this. While it's not mandatory to make it perfectly straight, aim to make it as straight as you can.

Step 3:

At the last 0.39inches (1cm) of the straight end of the bobby pin, use your pliers to create a hook that goes for at least 45 degrees. You can bend to any side of the pin as long as you hit the 45-degree angle.

If you don't have pliers, you can insert the tip of your pin into the lock you are trying to pick then bend it at the 45-degree angle

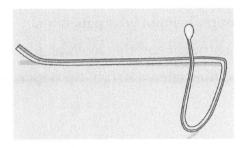

Step 4:

Use a second pin to bend a tension wrench

Bend a second bobby pin in the shape of an L. Use your pliers to grip the bent side of the bobby pin then overlap it by approximately 0.98 inches (2.5cm). Use a pair of pliers to bend the bobby pin at a right angle (90 degrees)

Your bobby pin picking set is now ready!

How to Make a Lock Pick From a Paper Clip

To make a lock pick from a paper clip, use the following steps:

Step 1:

Start by selecting metal paper clips that are at least 1.6 inches (4cm) in length to ensure the pick can reach the most interior part of the lock comfortably—plastic paper clips will break when you bend them.

Proceed by straightening the outer bend of your paperclip. When done, you should have a straight end that looks almost equal —in length— to the remaining curved part of the paper clip.

Step 2:

The second step is to twist the inner part of your paper clip. On the part of the paperclip that remains curved, there are two bends. Use your fingers and pliers to wrap the end of the clip around the straight part.

Although this step is not mandatory, it makes the paper clip easier to work with —and stronger, thus ideal for picking locks.

Step 3:

The third thing you need to do is create an M shaped bend.

Use your pliers to clamp the tip of the straight section of the paper clip tightly. Make sure you clamp it at about 0.79

inches (2cm). Use the fingers of your free hand to pinch the paper clip near the position where you are clamping the clip so that you can bend it an angle of 45 degrees. You can bend in any direction of your choice.

At this point, you can also go with the easier option of just bending a single hook, 0.39 inches (1 cm) long at a 45-degree angle at the tip of the end you straightened, or you can proceed to bend the M shaped option —which is way more effective.

Step 4:

Create three more alternating bends. Grip your pair of pliers around 0.20 inches (0.5cm) after the first end you made towards the tip of the clip. Create another bend of 45 degrees, but on the opposite side. Repeat the process two more times or until the shape looks like an M or W —depending on how you are holding your paper clip.

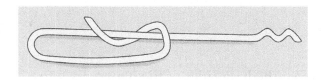

Step 5:

Use a second paper clip to create a tension wrench. Straighten out the outermost bend of the clip —just you did with the first one. Proceed by straightening out the innermost bend, which means you'll end up with two long parallel sides connected by a bend shaped like a U. The two sides should be almost equal in length.

Step 6:

Flatten the U shaped bend so that the two sides are touching. Do this by pinching the curve using your pliers and squashing it firmly until it is almost flat. Leave a small curve and ensure that you do not use too much force to avoid snapping the metal clip.

Step 7:

At the flattened out curve, grip your pliers at least 0.98 inches (2.5 cm) over the two sides, and bend at a right angle (90 degrees) either downward or upward. The clip should now look like a capital L that has an elongated vertical section.

Step 8:

Use your pliers to twist the long sides of the paper clip 2 to 3 times around each other. The more wraps you can make here, the easier your tension wrench will be to grip.

However, avoid making too many wraps because it may weaken your metal —it may even break off at the end.

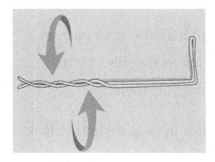

Your paper clip lock pick is now ready!

To become a master lock picker, you need to practice, which also means you need to prepare for lock picking sessions. Let's talk about how to prepare:

Chapter 6: How to Prepare For Lock Picking

Before you pick a lock, you must prepare for your current scenario. You can achieve this by inspecting the external appearance of the lock without using any tools.

Below are some steps you can follow to prepare for the lock picking process:

Check the condition of your lock

You should ensure that the lock is in a pickable condition before you begin, which ensures a smoother lock picking experience.

Investigating the overall condition of the lock will help you identify broken locks, rusted locks that may be frozen shut, or even foreign material in the keyholes. Such an evaluation will help you know whether you will proceed to pick the lock or look for an alternative.

For instance, if you determine that a lock is rusty, you can restore it to a pickable condition by applying a suitable lubricant such as WD40.

You should keep in mind that some lock conditions will make a lock insusceptible to picking no matter how skillful you are.

For instance, there's nothing you can do about a lock that has excessive rust or an old lock that has collected dust over many years.

Gather your supplies

Gather the lock picking kit, your basic tools, or your DIY tools that you need to start picking.

Regardless of whatever style of tools you have, the main things you need are a tension wrench, a lock pick, and a rake. Depending on the condition of the lock, you may also need a lock lubricant such as lubrication graphite or WD40.

Envision the locking mechanism

Depending on the type of lock you shall be working with, you should be able to paint a clear picture of how it interacts with a key to unlock.

Since you won't be able to see inside the lock as you pick it — which is usually the case with a lock picking practice set— having a firm mental image of the locking mechanism can be the difference between success and failure.

Worth noting is that the number of pins you have to pick inside the lock may vary. For instance, a padlock may have 3-4 pins, while a door lock may have 5-8 pins.

Another vital thing to note is that other locks, especially European ones, have their pins located at the bottom of their keyway instead of at the top. You should adjust accordingly based on the lock with which you're working.

To become better at lock picking, you need to practice and master various lock picking techniques. Let's discuss the techniques you should practice as often as you can:

Chapter 7: Lock Picking Techniques

Now that you are familiar with the different types of locks, how they work, and the tools you need, it's time to get to the practical part. This chapter shall teach you how to use the different techniques used to pick locks.

Single Pin Picking

Single pin picking, also abbreviated as SPP, is a lock picking technique where you find and set each pin at a time. It's one of the most basic forms of lock picking.

Although Single pin picking is not the fastest way to bypass a lock, it's a skillful and reliable technique. If you want to be a pro at lock picking, this is the best technique to focus on as you sharpen your skills.

The main idea behind Single Pin Lock picking is to use your tension wrench to apply light pressure to the keyway. After this, you will have to use your pick to push the key pins upward inside the keyway one at a time.

When each driver pin lifts above the shear line, the pressure from the wrench will hold it from falling back into place, thus allowing you to set the next pin. After you have all the pins set, the lock will open.

Below are detailed steps on how to use this lock picking technique:

Step 1:

The first step is to determine the direction in which the original key turns.

Insert your tension wrench either into the bottom or top of the lock's keyway. Use a single finger to turn it gently, thus applying tension (torque) to the plug. You will notice that the plug turns further on one side than the other. Take note that of that as the direction in which the plug should turn to unlock.

Step 2:

Next, use a pick to investigate the pins to get a feel for their alignment inside the plug. Do this until you can single out an accessible pin. Increase pressure to the pick slowly until you feel the springs on top of that pin give way. By increasing the pressure gradually, you will be able to test the resistance of the springs.

Some springs will require more pressure than others. Remove your pick from the cylinder and hold the image of the pins in your mind so that you can be able to track the position of solved pins in case you have to reset the lock.

Step 3:

Use a tension wrench to apply gentle pressure to the keyway. The goal here is to bring out a clear image of the position where the pins stop the plug from moving. Doing this will also allow you to get a sense of the tightness of the plug.

To start, insert the tension wrench into the top or bottom of the lock's keyway. Turn it gently, taking note of how the plug shifts, then reduce pressure on the wrench and repeat the process a few more times.

Step 4:

The fourth step is to identify the binding pin.

Use your wrench once again to apply pressure to the plug. Insert your pick into the keyway. Touch the pins inside the lock with the pick while applying tension. Release pressure from the wrench.

Repeat the process until you can identify a pin that is binding —has higher resistance than the others— when you apply light tension. That will be your first binding pin. The first binding pin will be harder to lift and stiffer than other pins inside the lock.

When you've identified the binding pin, be sure to maintain steady pressure on the tension wrench. Applying too little pressure can cause the pins to reset; on the other hand, applying too much pressure can cause your lock to freeze.

Step 5:

Use your pick to set the pins one at a time.

While still maintaining the same pressure with your tension wrench, use your pick to lift the binding pin gently until you hear an audible click or feel the plug turning slightly. Applying too much pressure to your tension wrench may end up causing your lock to freeze, hence forcing you to release the pressure and restart setting the pins again.

Slowly lifting the pin allows it to set easily. By practicing more, you will be able to increase the speed of this motion. Once you have the first pin successfully set, repeat the steps to find the next pin and proceed to lift and set it as it was the case for the first binding pin.

Continue locating the binding pins then lifting them gently to the shear line while maintaining the same pressure on your wrench until you have all the pins set. In most common locks, the binding pins are set from either back-to-front or in a reverse manner.

Step 6:

When you set the last pin, the lock will disengage fully and shift to an open state. At this point, you may have to apply a little more pressure to the tension wrench to allow the plug to turn. You can also use the pick —still inserted into the keyway— to exert a little more force. However, you should be careful not to damage the pick or even jostle the pins.

Raking

Also referred to as scrubbing or rake picking, raking is a lock picking technique used to open wafer and tumbler locks.

The main characteristic of this technique is the use of a pick that brushes light against the component of a lock, usually in an up & down motion, to stimulate a wide range of pin positions within a short time.

Follow the steps below to get started on using the raking method:

Step 1:

The first step is to use a pick and wrench to feel the lock.

Insert your pick into the keyway and feel the position of the pins lightly. Apply light pressure on one of the pins to test the stiffness.

Step 2:

Next, you need to use a rake tool to rake the pins.

Start by inserting your tension wrench into the bottom of the keyway. Using your finger, apply light pressure to the wrench in the direction where the key turns for that specific lock. Ensure the pressure you hold will be constant all through.

Insert your rake tool inside the keyway slowly and smoothly, ensuring you push it to the far end of the lock.

Apply gentle upward pressure, mostly focused on the tip of your rake, and snap the rake gently out of the keyway in a scrubbing motion while ensuring you bump all the pins.

If you had applied a reasonable amount of tension, then several pins will have set, and the plug will rotate slightly — the rotation may be un-noticeable to beginners.

Step 3:

The next part of the process is to repeat the raking process.

Insert your rake into the keyway once again and repeat the scrubbing motion. Repeat the process until you set all the pins. If you set the pins after scrubbing for 5 of 6 times, release tension from your wrench and start again.

Listen to the pins dropping inside the lock. If you don't hear anything, then it's a good indicator that you were using too much pressure on the wrench. As you repeat, try to alter the pressure you apply on the wrench slightly.

Step 4:

Once you apply the proper amount of tension and set all the pins on the shear line, the plug will allow you to rotate it fully and use your torque wrench as if it were the correct key.

Tips to help you achieve success with raking

As stated earlier, raking has a lower success rate than single pin picking. However, there are few tricks you can employ as you rake a lock to increase your chances of success. Below are some of the tips;

1: Pulsing

Pulsing is a trick you can apply to your torque wrench. Here, you gently pulse pressure applied to the wrench. Usually, pulsing uses more of a light tapping motion than a press. You should, however, note that this trick works best when applied for the first few pins and usually for a few seconds. Doing this allows you to know how the lock responds to your wrench and rake.

You can experiment with different 'pulse rates' and varying pressure. As you do this, take note of the feedback you receive from your tension rake and wrench. For instance, notice the tension of the pins & slight rotations of the plug. With a little practice, you will be able to interpret the feedback you receive.

2: Listen to feedback

With raking —and, in extension, all other lock picking techniques— reading and interpreting the feedback you receive from your tools is the key to success. Since you cannot see what is happening inside the lock, the feedback you receive from the tools helps paint a clear picture of what is happening.

Only by practicing will you be able to understand feedback from your tools. You should also work with a variety of locks and rakes so that you can learn the difference in the responses you get in different situations and from different locks.

3: Single pin raking

Sometimes you may find yourself in a situation where you repeatedly fail with just a few pins remaining (maybe 1 or 2). If this is your case, you can use your raking tool to SPP them. Just use the tip of your rake to feel the remaining pins –just as you would in the steps explained earlier for single pin picking, and position them in place one at a time.

Using A Pick Gun

As stated earlier, there two types of pick guns: the manual pick gun and the electric pick gun (EPG).

A lock picking gun usually speeds up the time it takes to pick a lock. You should, however, note that not all locks are susceptible to picking with guns –that includes locks that have serrated pins or pins that have been counter drilled and wafer locks. On the other hand, a pick gun is perfect for unlocking pin tumbler locks within the shortest time possible.

Here is how to use both the electric and the manual guns to pick a lock.

Manual Pick Gun

Here is how to use a manual pick gun

Step 1:

The first step is to install the appropriate needle into your lock picking gun

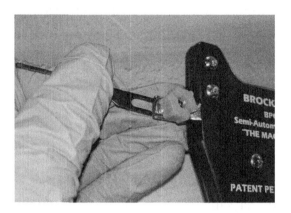

Pick guns usually come as a set pre-equipped with different needles that work as picks. To start, select a pick of choice, then unscrew the screw on the gun —the red part in the picture above.

Slide your pick into the needle slot of the gun and then tighten it to hold it down in place firmly. Once you have that done, your gun is ready for use.

Step 2:

Next, you need to secure your lock and insert your tension wrench

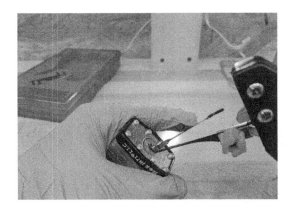

Use one of your hands to secure the lock, then proceed to place your tension wrench at the bottom of the lock's keyway.

Apply slight tension and insert the needle of your gun into the keyway so that you can feel the resistance of the plug and arrangement of the pins. As you insert the needle, ensure that you apply light tension on the wrench.

Release to reset the lock.

Step 3:

The third step is to insert the needle into the keyway to start picking

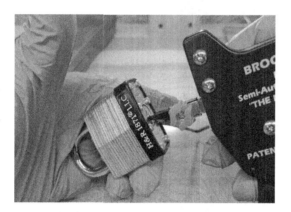

Push the needle into the keyway once more, ensuring it can reach all the pins. Apply slight tension to your wrench then pull the trigger on the lock pick gun. When you pull the trigger, a hammer inside the gun will release, thus forcing the needle to snap upwards.

Step 4:

Fourth, adjust the intensity.

Some pick gun models have a thumbwheel that you can use to alter the amount of snap-intensity. If the model you are using has this wheel, start using a low impact, then proceed to increase the intensity progressively if the lock does not open.

Keep in mind that adjusting the thumbwheel often requires practice. If you fail to set the pins, or if the lock does not unlock, repeat with a little more tension on the wrench. Continue doing this until the lock pops open.

The time it takes to open the lock may vary depending on the type of lock you have. If it fails, try to angle the needle of your gun slightly either upwards or downwards.

Keep in mind that when the needle of your gun snaps upward, it will force the driver pins out of the plug while the key pins remain in the plug, which will allow for a slight moment where the shear line becomes unobstructed. If you apply a proper amount of torque to your wrench, the plug will turn fully, and the lock will open.

Electric pick gun

An electric pick gun is one of the most popular lock picking tools. It's an upgrade to the manual snap gun

NOTE: The first manual pick guns were specially designed for use by the US police forces as a non-destructive and straightforward way to enter into a premise without much practice or training.

Electric snap guns are quicker and more capable —than manual pick guns— of picking locks successfully. The type of

EPG you will be using does not matter since most of them operate in the same manner.

Below are the steps to follow to use your EPD to pick a lock:

Step 1:

Because it's electric, the first thing you need to do is charge your EPG. Electronic pick guns usually have small batteries inside their bodies. These batteries can be removable or inbuilt.

To use the EPG, you will have to charge the battery first using the designated method for your specific model.

Step 2:

With your EPG on full power, attach the needle.

Make sure you choose a needle that's ideal for the lock you intend to pick and attach it firmly to your gun's screw using the tools provided —usually an Allen key or screwdriver.

From here onwards, all the steps are similar to those you would use when using a manual pick gun —explained above.

Important tips when using the EPG

When using your EPG, keep the following in mind:

✓ Pull the trigger in short bursts of approximately 2 seconds; constant action will not work. You should remove the needle from the keyway and rest the lock, hence eliminating false sets or freezing.

✓ Avoid pressing the trigger for extended periods because it can damage the motor on your EPG

✓ Practice on a variety of locks so you can gain experience using an EPG, which will allow you to know where it works and where it does not.

Picking A Lock Using Jigglers

As the name suggests, using jigglers has a simple concept. You've probably done it before without even realizing it.

A good example is when you insert a correct key into a lock, but it doesn't turn. In such an instance, the next step most people take is to jiggle the key inside the lock, up & down and side to side. You may also have tried pushing the key in a little bit and then out a little bit until the lock gives in. Does this sound familiar? Well, if you've done it, this principle forms the foundation by which jiggler keys work.

In lock picking, jiggling is the use of various movements inside the lock as a way to set the pins or wafers in the correct position, thus allowing the lock to open.

In the example above, when trying to unlock your door using the key, you apply a little pressure to the plug based on the direction in which the key turns when unlocking as you jiggle your keys. The aim of doing this is to turn the plug once the wafers or pins settle in the correct position.

In other lock picking techniques, we exert this pressure using a tension wrench. However, with jiggling, you exert pressure just as you would on a regular key; you don't need a tension wrench.

This technique usually works well with most padlocks that use the pin tumbler locking mechanism such as lockers, desks, post boxes, some padlocks, and older car locks.

To pick a lock using jigglers, all you have to do is select one of the keys in your 13 or 10-piece set and insert it into the lock you want to pick. Once you have the key inserted, jiggle it, move it, or even shake it as you apply pressure while turning left and right. If the first key doesn't work, try another key and repeat until the lock gives in!

Picking Combination Locks

A combination lock is a type of lock that uses a pattern of symbols (mostly numbers) to unlock. There are two types of locks in this category;

The single rotating dial

These types of locks are common because they offer mid to high-level security applications; you can find them used on safes, padlocks, and even lockers.

The type and quality of locks in this category may make some of them challenging to pick, even for professionals. Some, on the other hand, can be pickable based brute-forcing —or guessing— the combination.

Multiple dial lock

The use of this simple combination lock is common in low-level security applications such as travel bags, briefcases, and bicycle locks. This type of lock is very susceptible to picking or cracking.

Here, we shall focus on discussing how to pick this type of combination lock, specifically the three-digit lock.

These types of locks are unique since they do not use keys. To pick them, we will not be using any of the lock picking tools we've discussed. Instead, we shall look at how to unlock them by cracking the code

Cracking the code on a 3-digit combination lock

Before you can learn how to crack the code on this lock, you should first understand how it works, specifically its internal mechanisms.

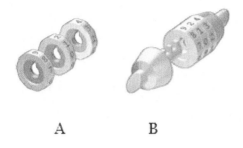

A   B

A combination lock has three dials that have notches cut into all the dials —shown in diagram A above; a pin that has a couple of teeth that hook onto the rotating dials secure the shackle of the lock —as shown in diagram B.

When you enter the correct code, the notches on the dials align with the pin's teeth, hence releasing the shackle. For instance, all the notches in picture 'A' have aligned, making the lock in an unlocked position. When you move or jumble the dials, the notches become misaligned, hence locking down the toothed pin.

Now that you've learned how this lock works, here're steps you can use to manipulate it.

Step 1:

The first thing you should do is apply upward pressure on the shackle. Here, you can use your hand or a piece of rope to achieve this. However, if the padlock does not lock onto anything, use a rope for better grip of the lock. The ideal length of rope is approximately 30cm long

Proper grip is essential here since cracking the lock will require you to apply an upward and strong force onto the shackle throughout the process, which is rather difficult to achieve using your bare hands.

This force is essential as it results in high friction on the dials, allowing you to hear a click when each dial turns to the right position. Applying pressure will also result in a slight upward movement of the shackle. If the lock you are trying to crack locks onto something sturdy such as a door or gate, you will not need the rope.

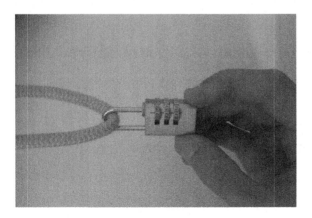

Step 2:

Secondly, find the first dial.

If you are going to use a rope, you should start this step by looping it on the padlock —as shown above. You will use this as a makeshift handle, which will give you a stronger and sturdier grip on your padlock, thereby making the procedure much more comfortable. You can even go ahead and tie the other end of the rope to something sturdy such as a metal bar.

With the rope in place, use your hand to clasp the rope tightly, then use thumb finger to push the top of the lock. Ensure you maintain this pressure on the lock throughout the process.

Rotate each the dials slightly with your free hand and feel the tension on each dial as you do so, which will help you identify the hardest one to rotate, which is your first dial.

Once you have found the first dial, rotate it until you hear a click, often accompanied by a slight upward movement of the shackle. Check that dial and take note of the number on that dial.

Continue rotating the same dial gradually to double-check the outcome. If it continues to make the same click on the same number for every rotation, then you have correctly figured out the first digit of your code.

Step 3:

Now you can move on to the next dial. Like in the previous step, rotate the two remaining dials slightly to figure out which one is the hardest to rotate. Repeat the same steps as earlier to find the second digit. Figure out the last code in the same way, ensuring you maintain constant pressure.

Step 4

As you rotate the last dial on the padlock, it will match up with the ones you had solved, and the shackle will be forced free, thus opening your lock

Shimming

In this lock picking technique, we use a tool called a shim, which is a thin piece of metal inserted in the gap between the body and the shackle of a lock to retract the spring-loaded latch that usually restrains the shackle thus opening the lock.

Just like any other type of lock pick tool, you can buy a professionally made shim or make one yourself using available materials such as aluminum cans —tutorial explained later.

Professionally made lock shims usually come in packs of 25 pieces, and a single pack can allow to pick up to 300 locks — based on the fact that shims usually damage easily because of their thin nature. They also come in several sizes to fit the contour on different locks.

However, worth noting is that not all padlocks are susceptible to shimming. High-security padlocks use locking mechanisms that make shimming impossible. For instance, some use bearings latch instead of the ordinary spring-loaded latch.

You can identify the type of latch used when the shackle is released. For the rounded latch, you will see a round indentation on the shackle instead of one shaped like a wedge.

Below is how to get started on shimming:

Step 1:

Start by ensuring that the type of padlock you have has sufficient clearance between the diameter of the shackle and the body of the shim, which will allow you to insert the shimming tool.

You should also determine whether your padlock is a single latch or double latch model. For the double, the latches will be on both sides of the shackle. For the single, the latch will be on one side —usually, the side that the notches of the key face when inserted into the padlock.

Step 2:

Wrap your shim around the lock's loop. Start by wrapping the shim around the vertical loop of your padlock, on the side that the lock opens. As you do this, ensure that the U-shaped side of your shim points downwards.

Use a shim that fits well into the diameter of your shackle. If your shim is too small or too big, then it might not be able to slide down into place.

Step 3:

Slide the shim down the shackle into the clearance. Push and twist it so that it goes as far as possible. When it goes down as far as possible, rotate it gently to allow the U shaped part of the shim to approach the latch from one side.

If you rotate it well enough without breaking your shim, then you will be able to disengage the latch from the shackle, making it possible to pull to unlock.

You might also hear a click sound to signify that the latch has disconnected from the shackle successfully. On a padlock that has weak latch springs, you might be able to slide the latch back from above without having to twist the shim.

Picking the lock with a shim may take a few tries. You might even rip off your shim in the process. When this happens, take another one and try again.

DIY Padlock Shim

If you are low on time and need to access contents locked in by a simple padlock quickly, then ordering the shims on Amazon won't be the quickest option. In this case, making a shim will be the best solution.

You can make one with things you already have lying around —such as the aluminum on a soda can. Below are the steps to follow:

Step 1:

Find a good aluminum can. Here, you can get away with just any beer or soda can. However, ensure the surface of the can has no ridges. It needs to be as smooth as possible to keep it from getting stuck as you slide it down the shackle.

Step 2:

Empty the can and rinse it with warm water. If you do not have an empty can lying around, then you can empty one from your fridge and enjoy a cold drink before you get started! When done, rinse out the residue from the can using warm water.

Step 3:

Cut off the bottom and top of the can.

To do this, use tin snips, a knife, or a pair of scissors. Cut along the part that forms the border between the sides and the bottom/top.

You may need to use a blade or knife to create a starter cut to allow you to get your scissors or tin snips in. As you do this, try to cut as straight as you can, and avoid cutting into the flat side of the can.

Step 4:

Cut a vertical line on the side of the can.

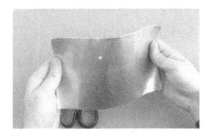

Look for a seam on the sides of the can that runs from top to bottom. If it has one, use it as a guide to cut open the can. If it does not have one, try to make the cut as straight as possible. Your aim here is to end up with a flat, rectangular piece of metal.

Step 5:

Now that your can is easier to work with, you should trim the bottom and top to eradicate the rough edges. If it is sticky with soda/beer residue, scrub it off well and rinse it off with warm and soapy water then rinse the cutting tool too.

Step 6:

Start cutting your rectangle in half, ensuring that it runs the long way of the rectangle. You will end up with two long strips. Cut the two strips into squares. Each square should be about 1.5 to 2 inches (3.8 to 5 cm) on either side.

As you do this, ensure that the edges of the squares are straight and smooth. Divide the squares in half using a marker. That should result in two equal rectangles.

Step 7:

Cut out an M shape

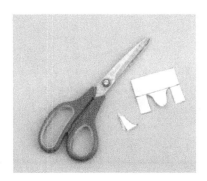

On one half of the line —the one you drew using a marker—, cut a design in the shape of an M —the aim is to create the U shape of the shim.

Cut out two humps with a little spacing from each other on both sides of the metal —shown on the image above. Ensure that the cuts are as smooth as possible. You should also make the humps rounded rather than pointy triangles.

Fold the uncut side of the square down in half; this part will be the handle of your shim.

Fold the two outer flaps of the M upward over to the top part that you just folded (the handle part). Crimp the handle using pliers.

Step 8:

Shape the shim

Here, you should round the tip of the bottom part of your shim so that it fits into the shackle of choice. You can achieve this by bending it around the shackle you want to pick or around a pencil or pen (that does not have ridges) then shaping it.

Be careful as you cut the shims. The smoother and straighter your cuts are, the better the shims will work. That will also allow you to cut out more shims from a single can as there will not be a lot of wastage.

Your shim is now ready for use on a padlock.

Picking Locks That Have Security Pins

Lock manufacturers have come up with different ways to devastate the efforts of lock pickers, including the feedback received or by trying to prevent the insertion of lock picking tools into the keyway.

Misleading feedback

As you have seen by now, feedback transmitted through your tools is a critical factor used by lock pickers. It helps you know whether the pins have set or not.

Knowing this, manufacturers use anti-picking pins, also referred to as security pins, to mislead you into thinking that a pin has set on the shear line. Manufacturers can either use the anti-picking pins as key pins or as driver pins (more common).

Below are some of the common security pins used by manufacturers.

Spool pin   Serrated pin   Mushroom pin

It's usual for most locks in this category to have either one or two security pins, while the rest are the standard types of pins. However, some manufacturers may use all driver pins as anti-picking pins of the same type or different types. Different combinations can make it harder to pick the lock.

The most common type of pin used as a security pin is the spool pin. The use of the mushroom and serrated pins is not common, especially in European cylinders.

How A Security Pin Works

As you can see from for diagram above, when you apply tension to the plug during lock picking, the anti-picking pin bends slightly, causing a slight rotation of the plug.

At this point, the security pin is still obstructing the plug. The feedback you receive gives you the impression that you have successfully set the pin at the shear line. The difference between really landing a pin on the shear line is easy to understand.

In the position illustrated in the diagram above, the security pin is depressed. That means you should apply pressure to the pin again using your pick. When you do, the plug will move back slightly to the locking direction because you have bypassed the groove meant for anti-picking.

How to Bypass Anti-Picking Pins

The concept behind overcoming anti-picking pins may seem very simple in theory, but the reality is that bypassing it requires a lot of practice to master.

It involves using very low pressure — only enough to hold it in place— on your tension tool as you apply pressure to the binding pin using your pick.

As stated earlier, when you apply pressure to your anti-picking pin, it will force the plug to rotate a few degrees. After this, you can vary the tension applied on your wrench to allow the plug to counter-rotate, thus allowing the security pin to push above the shear line.

You will know when it sets by the sound of a slight click and also the slight rotation of the plug to the unlocking direction. You can confirm that it is above the sheer line by pressing on the pin again. If it does not rotate in the opposite direction, then you have set it properly.

The amount of pressure you apply to the plug using your wrench is critical to your success at opening a lock baited using security pins. If you apply too much pressure, then you might not be able to feel the counter-rotation, which will hinder further progress.

For the rest of the process, you just have to repeat the process of finding the next binding pin and testing if it is a security pin until you can open the lock. If you get stuck, you probably made a mistake somewhere, and you will have to reset the pins and start from the beginning.

Picking Car Locks

With car locks, you can pick the ignition to start the car or the lock on the door. Many of the older models of cars use locks described earlier — like the pin tumbler lock that utilizes the same method.

If you have a newer model car, or if you do not have lock pick tools at the moment, you can use other techniques to bypass your car's locking mechanism.

Below is an example of a technique you can use:

Using a Coat Hanger Slim Jim To Get Into a Car

A slim Jim, also called a lockout tool, is a thin metal strip that measures approximately 24 inches (60cm) long and about 0.79-1.57 inches (2-4cm) wide.

You can buy a professionally-made slim Jim, such as the ones used by police officers to help people open their car doors.

However, in this part, we are going to learn how to make one using a coat hanger.

Step 1:

You will need to unfold and straighten the hanger, leaving only the hooked part at the end. Leave a length of about 0.5 inches that you will use as the lip of the hook, then leave the rest of the hanger straight.

This method is not ideal for cars that use automatic windows because such cars usually have a lot of wiring in the doors, and trying to use this method might end up cutting wires. However, you can pick the door on the passenger's side as it usually has less wiring.

Step 2:

If you still have the manual for your car, or if you can find it online, you should start by reading so that you can locate the locking pin and be able to access it with ease. Digging around may end up damaging your wiring.

Use your fingers to peel back the black rubber stripping slightly away from the window to reveal a gap between the outer metallic part of the door and the window.

Insert the straightened coat hanger into the gap, with the hooked side facing downward. You should be able to go down to a few inches without any resistance.

Step 3:

Once the hanger is inside the door, you should have enough room to turn it. Rotate it until the hook faces the inside part of the car, which will allow it to hook onto the lock bar in the door. To know which side the hook is facing while inside the door, consider marking one side of your hanger to help you know which position it is in when within the door frame.

Step 4:

Move your hanger around the insides of the door. Eventually, you will come into contact with a pin or bar that controls the locking and unlocking of the door. Push the hanger 5 cm —2-inches— deep, near the handle used to unlock the door from the inside of the car.

When you can identify and hook onto the bar, move it lightly from side to side or give it a gentle pull; if you notice the lock moving, then you have the right thing in your hook.

As you do this, you should note that:

- ✓ Different vehicles have different designs for the interior of the door. Therefore, this method may be ineffective for some models.

- ✓ Avoid using too much force when trying to pull the bar or pin upward, especially when you are not sure of what you have hooked; it might be a couple of wires.

- ✓ On some vehicle models, you might need to pull the locking bar or pin toward the back of the door instead of upward

- ✓ Keep the weatherstrip away from the area you are working on to avoid damaging it.

Step 5:

When you see the lock moving when you hook onto the locking pin or bar, you should try to pull it up or towards the back of the door to disengage the lock. If you hooked it correctly, you don't need to use too much force to achieve this. After you unlock the door successfully, gently pull out the coat hanger, and open the door to retrieve your keys.

Step 6:

Reform the hook on your coat hanger

Since you can't see what is happening inside the door, this method might be a little difficult, especially because different cars have different designs and working modalities.

With this in mind, you might have to keep changing the hook slightly, which might help you have more leverage on pulling the locking bar.

Chapter 8: Rookie Lock Picking Mistakes (& How to Avoid Them)

Sadly, committing mistakes is the only way to learn how to pick locks. Learning from your mistakes makes you better at what you do. Luckily, in this case, you don't have to learn from your mistakes.

In this chapter, you will learn some common mistakes that might derail your lock picking journey as well as how to avoid them.

Practicing only on one lock

During your early stages, you might find yourself committing the mistake of practicing using the same lock a couple of times. Doing this will give you the false perception that you are getting better at picking locks because the lock is getting easier to pick.

While there's a bit of truth to the notion that picking the same lock will make you better, it is more accurate to say that by picking the same lock is akin to memorizing how to pick that particular lock.

You should realize that every lock is different, with each one being like a puzzle. You can agree that the more you solve the same puzzle, the less skill it requires to complete compared to the first few times. When learning, skill is what you need to work on, not your memory.

When you repeat picking the same lock, you end up stuck on the particular feedback that the lock provides. That means if presented with a new challenge after using only one for some time, you would be expecting to feel the same feedback to pick it.

Always try experimenting with different locks. Try picking all the locks in your house and even getting more from friends or buying them cheaply from reclamation stores. Remember, it's better to pick 20 different locks once rather than pick the same one 20 times.

Picking locks that are too hard

Challenging yourself is vital to getting better at lock picking. However, trying to pick locks that are above your current skill level is only going to lead to frustration and a loss of interest in lock picking as a whole.

To avoid this mistake, you should;

✓ **Have a plan:** Create a detailed sequence of how you are going to proceed through lock picking. Do not jump from one technique to another. Master one method, then move on to the other. An excellent place to start is mastering single pin picking, which gives you a base of understanding of how everything works in a lock.

✓ *Take a break:* If you get stuck on one lock, it's advisable to keep it aside before frustration gets the better of you. Leave it alone for a couple of days or even weeks. During this period, practice on other locks or even go back to others that you found easier to pick for motivation. Keep in mind that even locks that seem too simple can present a challenge you didn't expect. When you are ready, equipped with a little more experience, go back to the lock you kept aside and try again to see if it gives in.

Using too much tension

Tension applied to a wrench is the most important aspect of lock picking, but often the most undervalued and overlooked.

Applying more tension usually amplifies the feedback you receive from your tools, including the vibration and sounds. That will help you know what is going on in the lock. However, when it comes to tension, there is a clear line crossed by beginners.

When you apply too much tension, you could end up bending or breaking your tension tool; it could bind the pins inside the plug that they cannot move, or you could end up breaking your picks.

When single pin picking, do not use too little or too much pressure on your tension wrench. With practice, it will become easier to know when you cross the line.

Using low-quality tools

Wasting money on cheap lock pick sets is another mistake many beginners make.

As stated earlier, the quality of your lock pick will affect the feedback you receive, its lifespan, and its effectiveness at lock picking the lock. If you choose a pick made from low-quality material, it might rust, bend, or break easily.

A quality lock pick set is an investment that may cost you slightly more than others in the market, but in the long run, a quality set will prove a worthwhile investment.

However, nothing about this means you should necessarily buy every type of lock pick tool out there. All you need are a couple of good rakes, hooks, and tension wrenches.

Relying too much on transparent locks

Getting obsessed with transparent locks is a common mistake most beginners make. These locks do not advance your lock picking skills; their purpose is to help you learn the concept behind picking a lock.

You should never use them for all your practice sessions. Practicing using a transparent lock will make you rely more on visual cues instead of feedback from your tools.

Focusing on the raking technique

Most lock pickers, including pro lock pickers, get excited by the possibility of popping a lock open quickly, a desire often satisfied by the raking technique.

However, keep in mind that raking does not necessarily work on all locks. Besides that, over-focusing on raking as a beginner will lead to a false perception of your lock picking skills.

As you begin your lock picking journey, try to work with as many lock types as possible. This way, you will discover that raking is ineffective on some locks, and you have to use other skills such as single pin picking to bypass some of the locks and develop your skill. Your lock picking skills should not revolve around one technique.

It's quite discouraging to have to go back to practicing with easier locks to refine your single lock picking skill while raking had you thinking you were a pro. It's even worse to find yourself struggling with the lock or even being unable to open the lock while knowing that you can unlock them with a rake in a few seconds.

To avoid this, work on different and more skillful techniques; don't focus on one and leave it at that.

Failing to practice regularly

Although some basic locks will open quickly, anything different from what you have become used to may come as a challenge, thus requiring a certain level of proficiency and understanding that you can only achieve from practice.

By practicing every day, even if it's only for 15 minutes per day, you will be able to preserve your newly acquired skill and build upon it at the same. Fifteen minutes a day might seem like too little time, but consistency is the secret to being better at anything.

Chapter 9: The Legality Of Lock Picking

Society has a general bias towards lock picking. Most people believe that owning lock picks can land you into great trouble, something that usually deters most beginners. That, however, is not the case.

In most states and countries, it's legal to own and use lock picks as long as the owner of the lock has permitted you to do so.

Possession laws

When it comes to possessing lock pick tools, to be declared illegal, most of the governments will require there to be proof of intent to commit a crime before you can be liable prosecuted. However, other states consider possessing lock pick tools to be 'prima facie, which simply means possessing lock pick tools is illegal because it is 'self-evident' that you were about to use them to commit a crime.

In such areas, to possess these tools legally, you need to be in a profession that's allowed to handle lock pick tools. For instance, you can be an automobile dealer or in the repossession industry. You can also be a certified locksmith or a lock distributor or manufacturer. You can also work for the government or be in law enforcement.

Consider the chart below as an example of possession laws in different countries around the world.

Country	Possession
Netherlands	Legal; there are no restrictions
Sweden	Legal
Poland	Illegal; certification required
Japan	Illegal; certification required
France	Legal; you must show intent
Finland	Legal; you must show intent
Australia (Queensland)	Legal; you must show intent

Purchasing and possessing lock picks is legal in 94% of the US, and most countries in the world. Below is a map of the US showing the legality of lock picking per state

Key

Lock Picks are legal by statute

Lock Picks are legal, based on lack of any clear statute

Lock Picks are legal, but it's better to be cautious

The Laws are vague and specific context should be deliberated

Conclusion

As stated earlier, practice is the secret to mastery. You need to practice a lot before you can become a pro at lock picking. Just don't go practicing on your neighbor's doors!